Praise for *In, (*

"...an enthralling, tru philosophical, emotional, is very strongly recom metaphysics and the contempiauve .... _ *Review* (Reviewer's Choice)   :s)f)f)k

"...an embarrassment of riches... one of the best books I've ever read." George Fisk (Cosmic Concepts Press publisher)

"...a poetic and stunning piece of work that will leave you inspired to contemplate your own existence in this world. ...Jack Haas has quite a tale to tell." Nancy Jackson (*Dog-Eared Book Reviews*)

"...lucid...and uncompromising. ...Read in awe." Benjamin Tucker (author of *Roadeye*)

Praise for *The Way of Wonder*, by Jack Haas

"...written out of reverence for the beauty in all life. ...especially recommended reading for students of comparative religion and personal spirituality." *The Midwest Book Review*

"...a most unusual, and powerful book." George Fisk (author of *A New Sense of Destiny*)

"Wow! ...What a glorious, uplifting, inspiring affirmation it is!" Jonathon Kerslake (editor, *Lived Experience*)

"This book really impressed me. ... a most stimulating read." Alicia Karen Elkins (*Gotta Write Network Reviews*)

Library of Canada Cataloguing in Publication data:

Haas, Jack, 1966-
  The dream of being : aphorisms, ideograms, and aislings / Jack Haas.

ISBN 0-9731007-5-3

  I. Title.
PS8565.A145D73 2003   C811'.6   C2003-910429-X
PR9199.4.H32D73 2003

Published by Iconoclast Press, Vancouver, BC and Hilo, HI.
Head office
Suite 144
3495 Cambie St.
Vancouver, BC.
V5Z 4R3
Canada

admin@iconoclastpress.com
website: www.iconoclastpress.com

For my father,
a man full of generosity,
strength, life, and dreams.

aphorism: a terse statement or insight.
ideogram: an idea expressed in symbols.
aisling: an Irish term for the poetic description of a vision or a dream.

Contents

* bold text are
ideograms

4

Part I: The Nigredo

"There is a dream, and it is dreaming us."
Kalahari Bushmen

"When we die, we return to the Dream world."
Maori cosmology

"My homeland is unreachable except in dream."
Huang Ching-jen

"You are an eternal dreamer, dreaming non-eternal dreams."
Neville

"There is no way out! Don't you see that a way out is also a part of the dream? All you have to do is to see the dream as dream."
Sri Nisargadatta Maharaj

BIRTH

the dream of being

It would be despairing if you existed only as a character in another person's dream, for the other would certainly want to be awakened. And yet to awaken them would amount to your own dissolution. So you would not awaken them; you would rather exist in a dream than not exist at all. But what if this dream is a nightmare of your self? That is: would you keep them sleeping, if the dreamer dreaming your being ...was you?

We dreamt that we were dreaming, and then that we were dreaming that we were dreaming, and then that the dreamer was not the dreamer but the dream. In the end there was no dreamer, only the dream of a dreamer; a dream dreaming a dreamer. We do not dream, we are dreamt. The Dream dreams the dreamer, then the dreamer dreams, then the dream of the dreamed dreamer dreams, and so on. The dream dreams the dreamer, the dreamer does not dream the dream.

Dream on dreamer.
You are but a dream-catcher.
And you are caught.

the wall

A long time ago a person was chased to a wall and then slain before they could dig through it. And then came many others, similarly chased, similarly doomed to be slaughtered while digging at the same spot. Until after a great duration the mass of indistinguishable corpses created a tremendous labyrinth hindering both hunter and prey.

Now, perhaps you are within this interminable structure. Perhaps even leaning against that very wall- a barrier attacked with bleeding fingers and panicked charges. You can sense the danger, the confinement, and the hidden anguish forming the foundation of it all. Yet you do not consider digging. Not until they are upon you.

light

In the infinite expanse of unknown darkness, there is indeed a light, but it is unfortunately only a residual candle-end; a little flame fluttering on a charred, lifeless wick which floats sputtering in a vanishing drop of impure wax. And this you must solicitously carry about in the darkness, searching for the fatty remains of other spent candles that might feed your dying flame. Yes, there is a light, but it is barely discernable even though it be in your grasp. Oh, it is so dim and precarious, it hardly sheds enough light for the duties you must ceaselessly perform, in order to keep lighted the light.

the treasure

It is as if someone left their treasure for you to guard while they had to go away. But now you can't remember when they said they would be back. You want to leave, to attend to other things, but then who'll guard the goods? You must stay, or convince another to take on your duty until the owner returns, whenever that is, whoever it is. In fact you have never even met the owner, but were simply handed the task by another who was handed it by another, and so on, back so far that no one can remember whose treasure it is. No one even knows what it actually is. Still you must stay until another will take your place. That is all you are sure of. You must stay.

It's like holding a lottery ticket which you didn't buy and which you don't know what the prize is, nor when it will be announced. Nor even where. You know simply that the only thing worse than having a losing ticket, is losing a winning one.

11

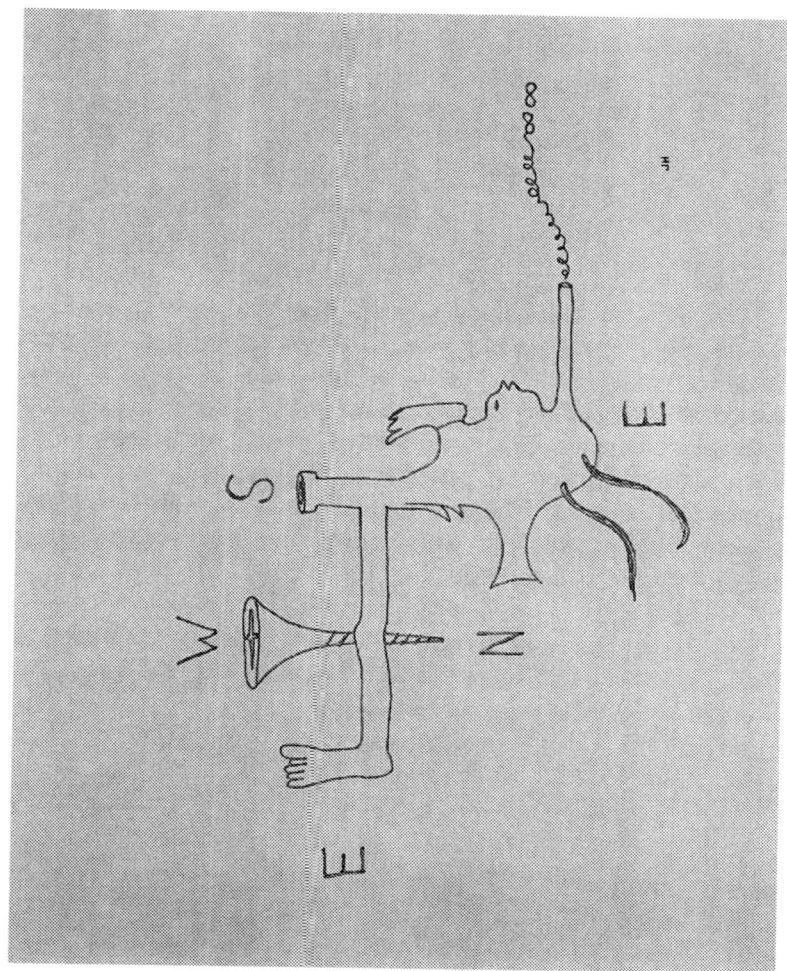

DIRECTION

the secret

It is as if all along you are excluded from a secret of which you happen to also know. This placates nothing, however, because you do not know that what you know is the same as the secret from which you have been excluded. You struggle because you cannot remember what you are trying to remember, even though you have already remembered it; you cannot remember that what you remembered was what you were trying to remember- and so you are doomed, because you will never remember what you have not forgotten.

It is as if you are given the secret knock for heaven's gate. Unfortunately you are not told whether it is the knock for those to be let in, or those to be kept out.

the self

Like volcanoes do we emerge, built up and destroyed by our own eructations. Life is naught but existential exhibitionism- the show-and-tell of nothing's somethingness; we suffer to become, then we become, then we suffer because we will cease, then we cease; yea, we force the separate self to exist and then grieve that it must die.

To manifest oneself intentionally upon life is naught but existential exhibitionism; the show-and-tell of nothing's somethingness. Self is the last nail in its own coffin. Only the obscure person is safe from their own self.

One gets tricked into existing- cajoled by the ubiquity of insufficient potentialities; a nobody clinging to somebodiness.

Self is *the* temptation.

A scaffolding is raised around a structure in order to repair it. Eventually, however, the inner structure crumbles and is forgotten. Generations later only the tottering scaffolding remains. But by then it is called self.

the exile

It is as if we are not wrecked, but intentionally cast onto this inhospitable shore- as if we are not stranded but chosen to stalk wildly into this land with the knowledge that we were sent, but without the knowledge of why we were sent here- and that is to know the lonely grief of duty, without remembering the call.

Every moment is an improvisation, for no one has seen the script. The director is nowhere to be found, and the rest of the cast is a bloodthirsty mob of petty, ostentatious insufficiencies. And only because of this- because you are bored and pissed off, and because you know neither the plot, nor your part; it is only because of this that you eventually picked up your bags, and walked out of the theatre.

The test is this: Anyone who does not refuse to take the test, fails the test.

sowing the seeds

You appear to yourself as if with convicted intention: you have a large basket in your hands and you are ceaselessly looking up, waiting for the fruit to fall. But really you are only delaying the inevitable. And you will starve if you continue to tolerate your hunger, for what falls to you is sparse, and fertile ground is a place within which you have never gardened.

Gardener, you are the garden.

An unknown seed is carried at one's warm breast great distances, only to reach arable land and find that along the way, because of that very warmth, it has sprouted, and died.

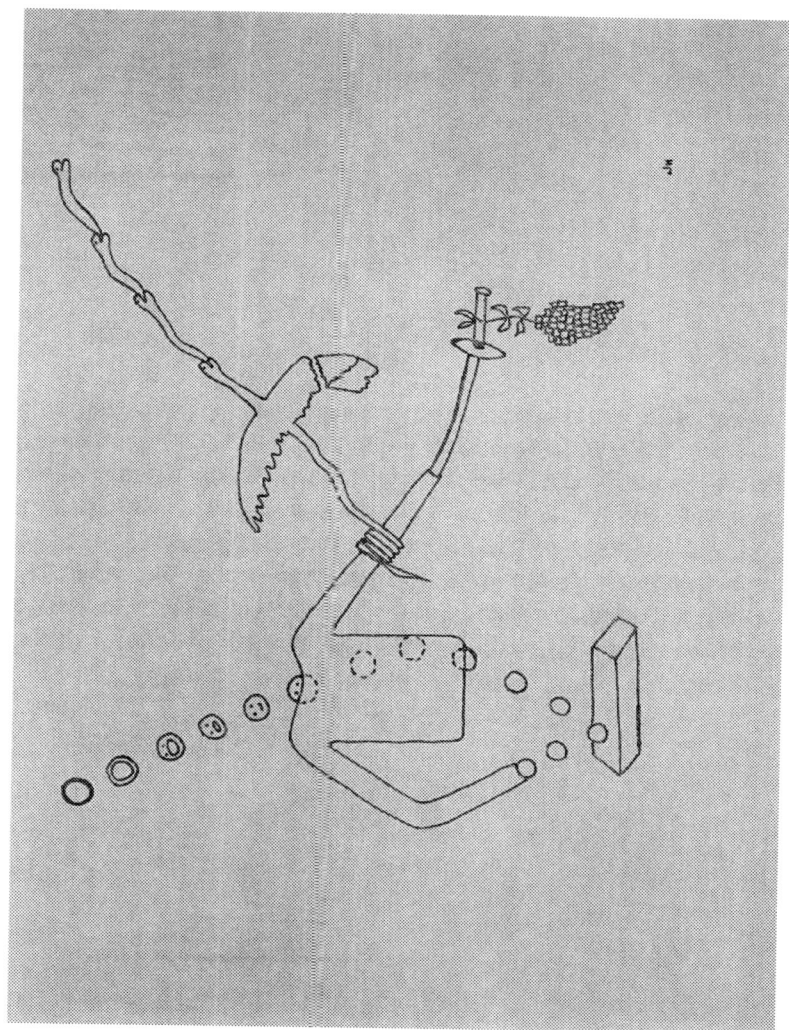

SPIRIT

the messages

The various Kings and Queens of the infinite land only thought they were communicating to each other, while, all along, the royal messengers had instead been creating and delivering their own forged notes between the unwitting monarchs, and had, in the course of that real and unreal eternal dialogue, never once taken the actual imperial message from one leader to another. Thus those worthy and ignorant Kings and Queens of the land forever hated, feared, and applauded one another, without ever hating, fearing, or applauding one another.

life

A cow, who understood that its destiny was to go to the slaughterhouse, intentionally ate less grain than necessary to make it fat with meat, and thus fit to be killed. Yet it also ate enough grain so as not to be thought sickly and thus also killed.

Every year the healthy cows were led to slaughter, and the infirm ones were destroyed, and the farmer kept only the one cow not fit for the butcher, yet who still was bearing promise, and that cow lived on between death and death, ever wise, ever hungry, ever strong.

It is the nature of the epiphyte, a plant which grows without soil, high on the limb of a tree, that it lives off what the earth produces, but is not attached to the earth.

Indeed it is harder to be nourished without being soiled, than to be soiled without being fed.

futility

I

Like how a tropical tree planted in a temperate garden will still grow and live, and take in the sun and soil, and yet will never attain to its true height, and will die without knowing what it is to be pollinated, to blossom, and then to bear fruit. Like that tree that is no tree there is a proximity to unattainableness, a closeness which is the greatest distance apart we can endure. Just as with all the spermatozoa who arrive at an egg too late- for, after all, only one crazed, writhing life gets in, and the membrane impenetrably hardens- these are the superfluously competent, who nudge against impossibility, as if to beat themselves on their losses.

II

We are the dogs Pavlov starved, intentionally, before he rang his bell; we drool for salvation, having been denied the mundane; we dream of a banquet that may never be eaten, but that we might fill our beings with hunger.

III

A person once placed a stuffed hawk in the middle of their lawn to scare away the frenzied jays. It was successful, though the possibility of scavenging from the predator then attracted twice as many crows.

effort

Within us is a groundwater tide which rises and falls, swells and retreats, offers and takes, rushes and recedes, and though it beats upon no conspicuous shore, nor betrays a crash of surf, nor any breakers by which we might divine the medium in which we are obliviously drowning, and which we obliviously are, still like a man who struggles and struggles in quicksand, thrashing wildly to get out, who soon realizes that ultimately he is powerless, we know only after taking our last, desperate breath, that flailing in the mire ...that struggling was a mistake.

Yea, though his strength increases to Herculean proportions ...a drowning man still drowns.

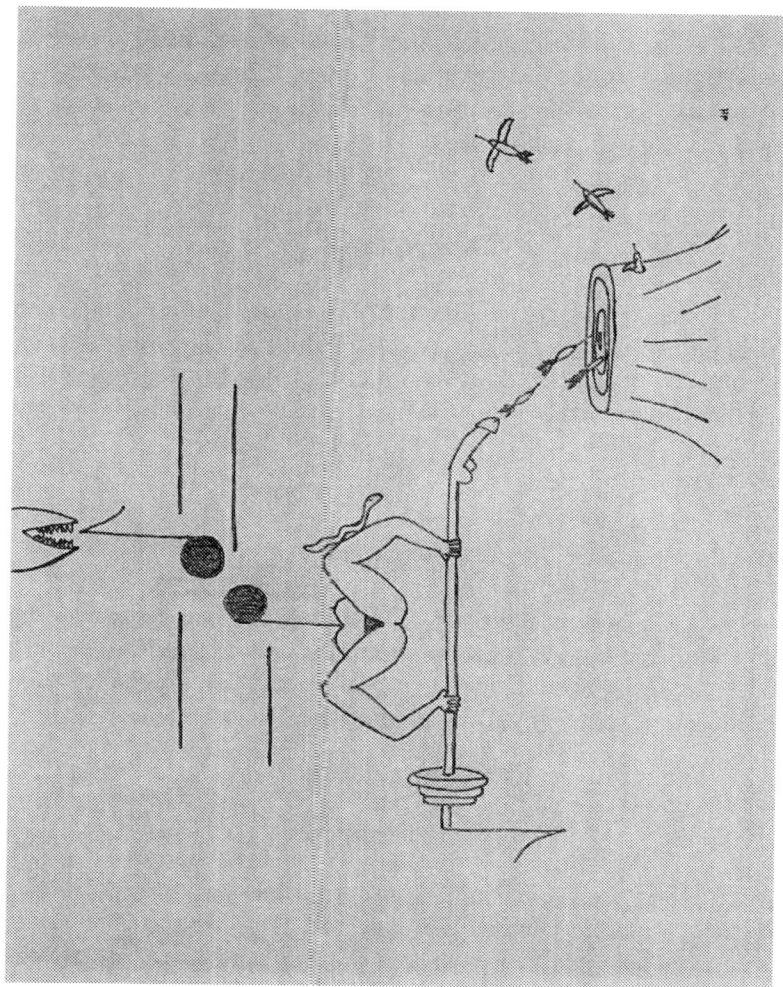

SOUL

25

the hunter

The musher has dropped his whip and fallen from the sled. His leg is caught in the tangle, and he is pulled desperately along the ground by the now directionless reins. His screams only drive the hounds further.

the hunted

There is an African antelope so timid that it can be slain without even aiming; the mere report of a rifle, or a fire-cracker, or the sound of its hoof coming down upon brittleness, or perhaps even its own heartbeat ...and the shocked beast collapses.

the game

The sore and bloody, velvet eruptions are cursed by the stag who has not yet heard the howls of wolves, nor felt the fury of their jaws- phenomena for which it will have need of such burdensome antlers in order to insufficiently defend itself.

and the catch

The case remains of the eagle which swooped down and clenched upon too great a fish, and so was taken under the water and deep enough that neither its great wings, nor beak, nor mighty talons could ever again liberate it from the sea.

self knowledge

You spent your days harvesting the abundance whose seed fell from misunderstanding. You sought no cultivation of the heart, only a fallow conception, where idea progresses unnaturally, where thought uproots all growth and plows away all fertile possibility; where thorn succeeds thorn, until the blinding thicket constricts all movement, ensconces every happening, and thought dwindles back into the earth, choked in the spasms of meaning's plenitude, and plenitude's failings.

You are this person, bound by an abundance of dreams and anguishings. You eat what you have not slain, you slay what you do not eat. You have nothing in yourself except the harvest of another person's scythe. And that other is also you, but you know it not, and so your life remains unforgiven.

Today is yesterday's failure; your mint is broken, and you have not yet stamped enough coins to repair it.

a fool

There is a person who barters for their life's contingency. This is done without intention, and so occasionally succeeds. However, if they were to claim the furrow from the plow, the plants would castigate their hunger by filling it beyond want, and by starving it beyond need, as if cursing life's fecundity by scattering precious salt into a brackish sea

This person is a fool. Not because they believe that knowledge is anything more than the labeling of enigmas, nor for imagining that knowledge is greater than the enigmas themselves. No, they are a fool, instead, for assuming that truth transforms an enigma into knowledge ...and not the other way around.

salvation

There is a withered and weary, crotchety old man who you never have met nor heard of, yet who remains faithfully outside of your door, for reasons you cannot fathom, every evening, frantically battling lunatics and beasts away until, come morning, the foes are all diminished and he lies wrecked and dying.

This happens every night, while you obliviously slumber, comfortable and safe, knowing nothing of beasts nor madmen intent upon your demise, nor of a frightened and lonely, battle-weary knight who hopes for nothing more than the day when there will be no more marauders, and the fighting will finally end, so that he can die, because you can live.

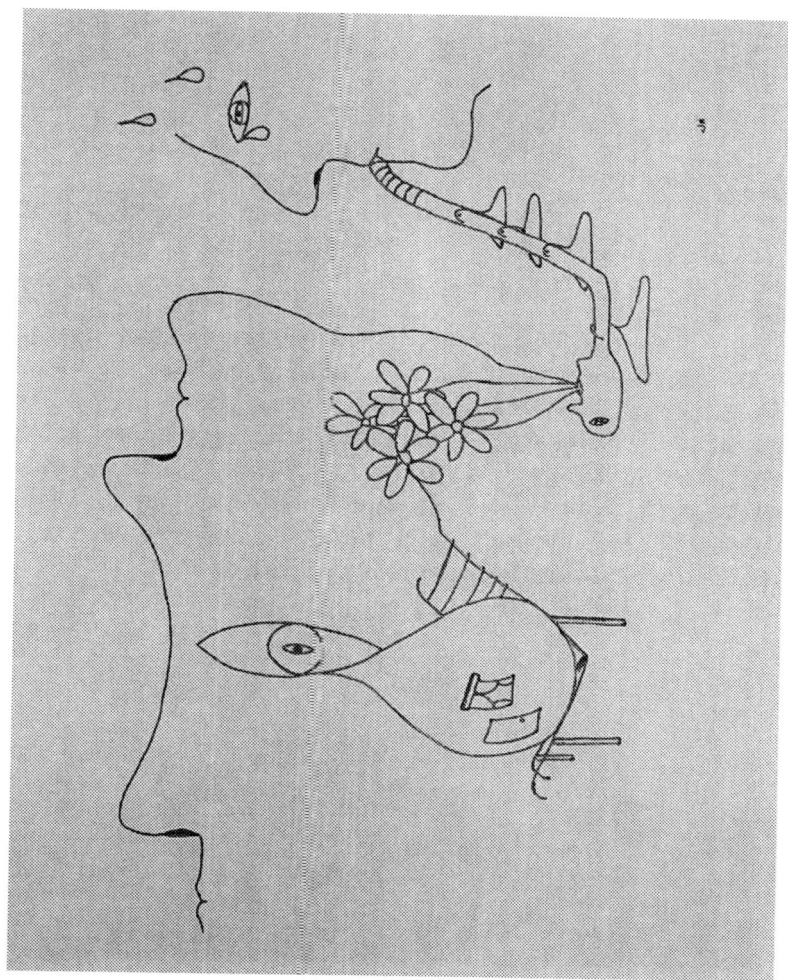

GROWTH

lost bees

There are bees in every hive with inherent imperfections: they cannot navigate from the directions given by others. They fly off everywhere. They are always getting lost. They never gather much pollen. Yet, by an incongruous twist of fate, these bees can still dance directions to others. And so they occasionally return from their misguided wanderings with delirious gospel of what they have found. Good god, what they have found! It is the lost bee who finds new flowers.

catechism

      A person, deciding on which brand of soap to buy, imagines it is their choice to be clean- so why, then, are they dirty? If you are a lion-tamer, why then are you locked in a small cage surrounded by uncaged lions? How long will a person hide from a frightening beast which has not yet hurt them? How long will they hide from one that has? If the plane is going down, why polish the windows? Is it better to be under house-arrest, or to be locked out? Is it safer to be a weak man behind a bolted door, or a strong man exposed in an opening? You can tame a wild beast, but can you untame a domestic one? Is there a term for fear of oneself? And is this term ...fear? Do we simply beseech a greater intensity of the incomprehensible lives we continue to obliviously lead? Are we merely the terror of an ephemeral remembrance; a dream waiting to be forgotten? In ecclesiastic winter, how shall we judge a tree by its fruit? What if acknowledging our debilitating limitations is the thankless pinnacle of our inadequate beings? Is this the zenith required for adherence to a doctrine concerning the inevitability of itself? If we find within ourselves the prolonged adoration of whatever mystery prompted our becoming, will that adoration, then, be suspect as the original intent of the prompter? Could we paint round rocks into soccer balls and, leaving them on a field, define transgression as the moment just preceding folly: the first presumptive kick? Are we simply the angst of ancient windows, forced to view recurrent folly with tedious disgust? Is this atmosphere of dread and boredom merely the concomitant fallout of an evolution overtly impatient with itself? And are we at the final stage of our apocalyptic lives, where we can abdicate our will, but not our suffering?

the other side

You are what is behind the locked door. You can wait all you want, but you will always be there, waiting and wondering if whatever is behind the door is a similar somethingness, waiting behind a door to find out what is behind the door- waiting to find if they *are* the waiting. If that is the case, then the door can never be opened. For that which is waiting always must wait. Therefore you either know everything that you are, or nothing that you are. But if this is not the case, then what are you waiting for?

Perhaps you must bash your way through a strong, resilient door with naught but your hands and body. A task which almost destroys you, and which, upon success, you find that there lies on the other side, another, similar door.

And so, bloodied, broken, and weary, you eventually begin to attack this next door, wrecking yourself to have knowledge or be free. And when finally your mangled life wins this door, there stands a similar one behind it.

And so it goes that you pound and thrash your way through countless doors, until, seeing no end, you stop and struggle no more, eventually dying on the wrong side of what you do not know is the last door.

Yea, the door which you cannot see through; the door which you come upon and from which you turn away; the barrier towards which you do not set to sedulously chiseling through; that door is the only one where you are waiting on the other side; that door has killed the you who was to dig past it.

a tool

What will you do now, if you are not there to do it? You have been given no means. A scream will only shatter the glass walls around you. Try, quivering hero, try. Swing your plastic sword into the night. Everything you have ever, and will ever be told, everything you know or will know, it is all a lie, all of it. Muster all of your forces and charge, or else turn around and don't give a damn. Either way, you shall never get out, and you shall never get in.

And yet, if you are chiseling through what you know not, towards what you know not, for reasons of which you are not certain, then why are you chiseling?
Simple ...you are a chisel.

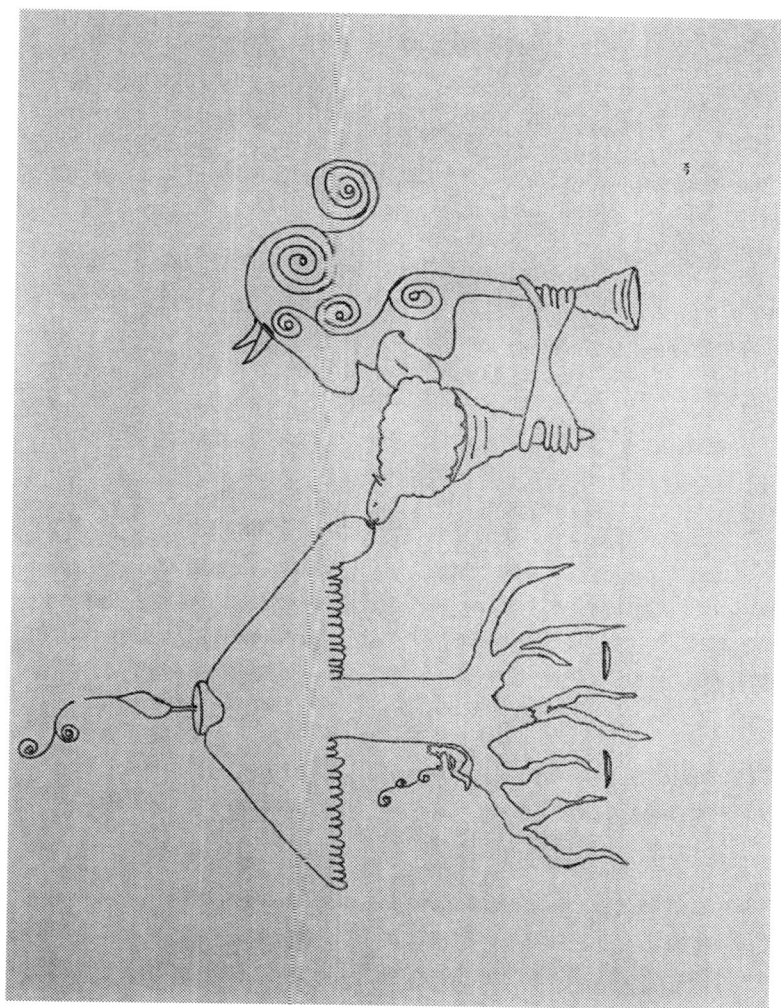

Part II: The Albedo

"Dreams! Maybe there were dreams before there was anything else; maybe there were dreams before there were people to dream them."
Russell Hoban

"The world is Vishnu's Dream."
Hindu Lore

"... a vast dream, dreamed by a single being, in such a way that all the dream characters dream too."
Shopenhauer

"Hawaiians say that the truth to all reality lies in the dreamtime of our imagination. ...This viewpoint is shared with other tribal peoples, such as the Aboriginals of Australia. They call the greater reality from whence comes all, the 'Dreamtime'."
Pila Chiles

"...shamans also hold the exceptionally subtle idea that life is a dream; that, in fact, we dream our lives into being."
Serge Kahili King

"Were it not for a dream dreamed by a forgotten race I would not suffer your sun to rise upon my patience, nor your moon to throw my shadow across your path."
Kahlil Gibran (voice of *Jesus*)

mining

If you should choose, instead of smashing through the doors, to wander aimlessly through the limitless labyrinth, what then? What is the use of directions when one is within an insoluble maze? How is it possible to make progress, if a person progresses not by making the right choices, but, rather, the right mistakes?

Should one abandon all hope of ever finding, and instead proceed to get more lost? If one runs and runs, and yet still comes upon nothing, then what is one to say? One has certainly gotten somewhere. Or is truth is simply the most well lit routes of all digressions?

You run from one dead end to another, you turn around, you run again, on and on and on, always imagining you're making headway, or not. You don't know. For there is no depending on ancient tunnels and crumbling passageways. You are too far gone to retrace old routes towards antiquated ontologies.

Alchemist of the soul- how does one transform a turd into chocolate? Simple, do not eat the chocolate.

doing

A football coach once declared that in order to tackle a strong opponent coming straight at you, you should not aim just for the man, but instead you must aim for a spot three feet behind him, only then will you have the inertia and power to take him down.

not-doing

None are ever killed going over the waterfall. It is because of the frantic, fruitless struggle, when one swims desperately trying not to go over; it is because of this- because of the futile effort at the crest- that none have the energy to swim safely to the welcoming shore.

punctuated existence

...	(one is a born continuation)
...;	(connected and detached)
...;?	(which questions itself)
...;?!	(and is shocked by that questioning)
...;?!.	(occasionally it ends there)
...;?!...	(or it continues)
...;?!...( )	(continues to something)
...;?!...(?)	(but to what?)
...;?!...(?)!	(one is shocked again by such continuation)
:...;?!...(?)!	(so one looks backward)
( ):...;?!...(?)!	(but to what?)
?( ):...;?!...(?)!	(one questions again)
!?( ):...;?!...(?)!	(one is startled again)

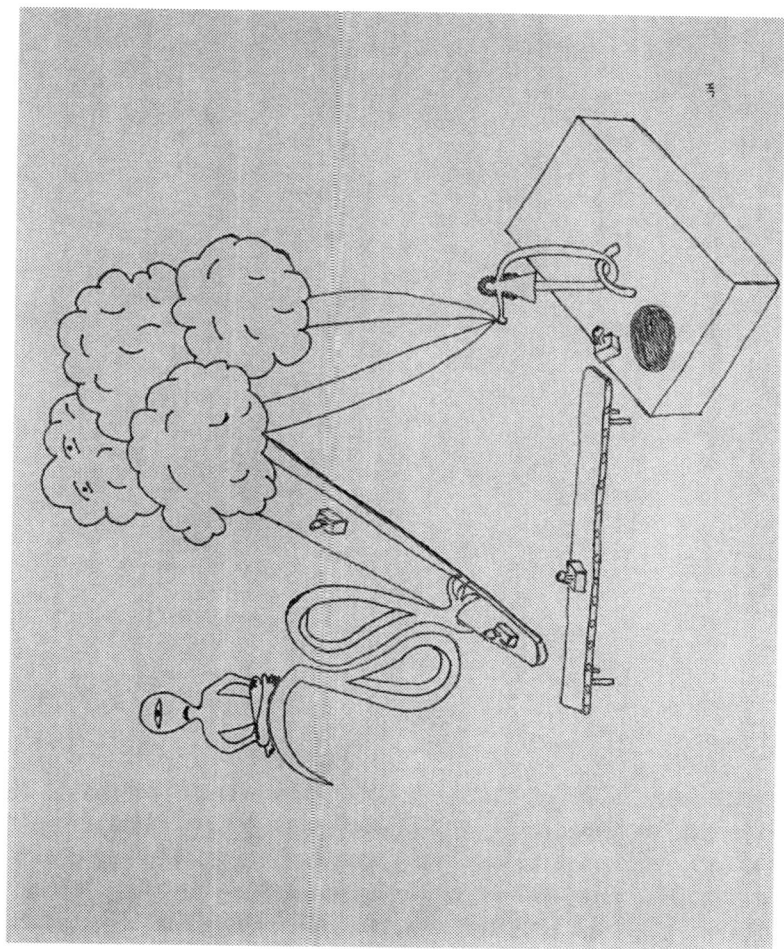

INCARNATION

an asterisk

```
( )
( ),
(( )),
((...)),
((...!)),
((...!)!),
((...!)...!),
((...!)...!)?,
((...!)...!):?,
((...*)...!):?,
(("...*")...!):?
("( ...* )..."!):?,
("( ...* )...!"):?,
("( ...* )...!)":( )?
("( ...*? )...!):"( )?,
("( ...* ?!)...!):(!)?",...
```

*Life is an asterisk, denoting an explanation to follow, in an obscure, cryptic text, which continues to be anonymously written. And yet there is no text, only a prologue explaining what will not be said, and an epilogue reaffirming nothing. We are life's shocking confessions, cryptic lexicons, recondite testimonials, and incoherent filibusters full of spit and tears, awe and approbation. It is not the meaning, but the mystery of being which we must discover; truths do not demystify the world, they remystify it.

old souls

There is all this talk of 'old souls'. Everyone respects old souls. Everyone wants to be an old soul, which is nothing but a bunch of prideful bunk. For, if you are an old soul it simply means- you are responsible for the mess all around us. What have you been doing all this time? Murdering? Raping? Cursing, preaching, hiding, and all the rest of it? What a heap of pathos you have been dragging hopelessly behind you. You're it. What is there to be proud of?

Perhaps it is far better to be new. Brand new. Eternally. At every moment.

You can have your false calm and old wisdom. It's all a romantic lie. The longer you sit on the toilet, the less your own shit stinks.

the runner

Neither wild nor tame, we are feral lambs roaming mad between fence and forest. Belonging nowhere, abandoned everywhere. Bolting without recognition, without reason, without need. Just bolting. Here, there, everywhere, and none. Terrified, ferocious, and crazed like alien beasts lost from their herd, shepherd, territory, instinct, and wonder.

the flyer

We are but thin albatrosses, forever struggling above the infinite sea, though we do not belong forever in the sky. We belong to what cannot be found- land enough to rest our weary souls upon. Oh, we are great flyers and all, and indeed we could remain eternally on wing. But it is only because there is no place to land without drowning in the froth, or being consumed by one of the monstrosities lurking rapaciously below in the deep, that we continue to beat indifferently into the gusts, and fly away wasted, with nowhere to sleep, to dream, to be.

We are the drones not killed by the Queen; we have consummated, and conceived, but we were not consumed. And so we now fly about, here, there, everywhere, and none, for no reason but because we have no reason. And, well, because ...we can fly.
Reason cannot fly. That is our reason for flying.

the flight

We circle the world like hawks scanning for sustenance; like hawks which search and search and, finding nothing, slowly wither away, dissipated of intent, forever cursing the carrion temptations.

Atrophying amongst the wind's indifference, soaring higher and higher, we become weaker and lighter, until it seems we can never fall back to earth, but are blown away, lofted upon the feverish gale- as massless corpses of feathers, futily embraced by the sky's numinous acceptances.

the flown

Like the lonely and terrified, the lost and forgotten, the preponderance of an extinguished occurrence, the dispossessed yet possessed, the estranged, residual, persevering aftermath; the insubstantial, the past and the going, plunging forever into the infinite; we are the eternal, irresolute, indisputable, insufferable light ...of stars long dead.

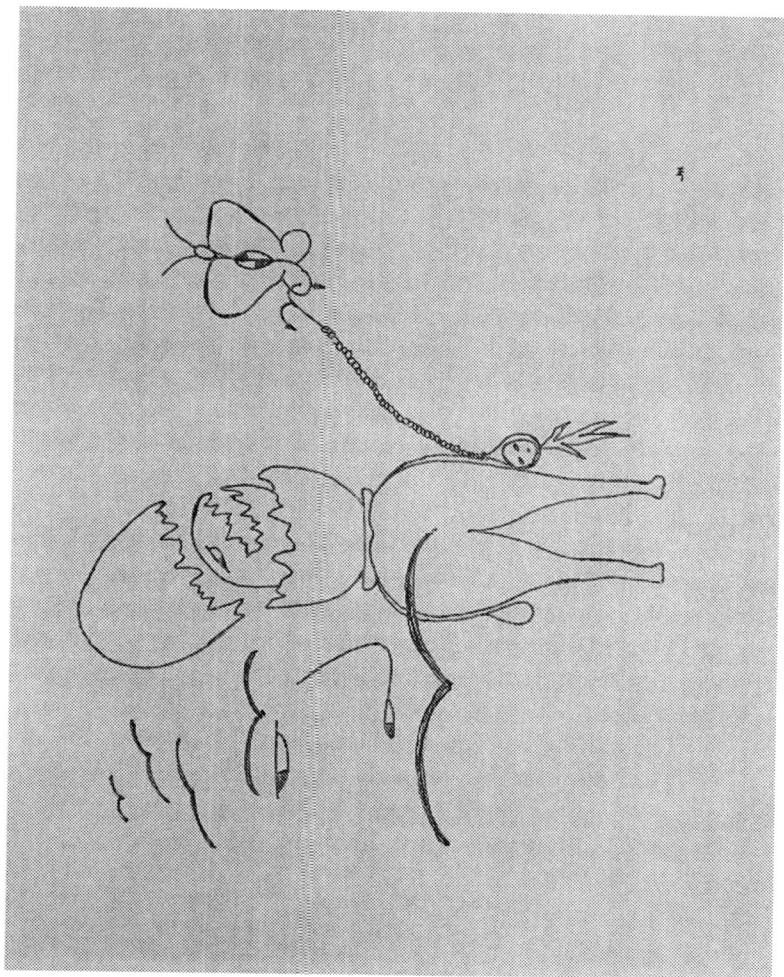

uncaught

All creation has arisen out of one thing- boredom. The God which we are and don't know it was so bloody tired of nothing ever going on that God invented a whole cosmos simply to relieve that divine, eternal torpor. And that's why it all seems meaningless- because just as a person might sit doodling on some scrap paper at the kitchen table, while occasionally looking absently out the window to watch the day go by, anything like that, done out of boredom, has no purpose except as a jumbled mad miracle. And perhaps therefore it's now time for us to accept our initial, fatuous arbitrariness, and get on with some purposeless jubilation.

Only when we have regained the capacity to live without reason will we meet the universe at its quintessence. To not understand, to not expect it to make sense, to realize that it is all implausible, marvelous, incomprehensible, is to accept our ignorance of the miracle we have accepted. To accept ignorance is to create awe.

The pawn alone can turn into a queen.

Yea, the light that shines in man is the same that causes him darkness; a tiny candle burning so bright in the night, that he cannot perceive the immaculate stars glistening and dancing all around.

in the ether

Indeed it is hard to have no grounding, no specific interest, no intention, no understanding of what one is, or what one is supposed to be. There is no certainty to begin with, no orientation point, only the vast amorphous madness of being, whipping and spinning us about from impossibility to impossibility, never touching down, but blowing us hither and thither, like winds driven and tossed in the wind.

Hard indeed to follow the course we cannot avoid taking.

Ah, how the spirit soars at the expense of its footing, though we must cease to be petrified, as the world drops mercilessly out from under our feet.

Drifting, and self-forgotten, fluid in infinity, we groove into the chaos. Swerving into the pleroma, we rejoin the legion of cosmic wanderers.

Yea, though we fall and fall and fall, struggling every unpredictable step of the way, eventually we become more adept at living out of balance ...as seamen will tell you.

messiah

When a newly caught fish is thrown into a boat already loaded with many others, made docile over time, this new one flops and thrashes about wildly, mad at its terrible plight, and the others, revivified by the frantic energy of the new fish's fight, begin, from the torpor of their slow deaths, to also flop and thrash about wildly, and so all are lifted strong by the contagion of freedom and are now able to sink the sinkable ship.

Ships sink. Dead men float.

Silence is not the intended outcome of screaming. But it occurs.

the fledgling

You were trying to complete a puzzle without having first collected all the pieces. You wanted to make sense of what is senseless. You wanted to finish what you forgot you had not started. You sought to reduce yourself towards an irreducibility, to be conscious of vacant ecstasies. You strove to dissipate and to occur, to hope without needing, and to run without fear. You imagined you were living in two worlds, when actually you were dying in both. You wanted to return to where you never had been. You sought freedom from seeking. You were earnest to be still. You wanted to be. You wanted to not-be. You wanted to detach from detachment, to cling to not-clinging, and to heroically surrender. You were trying to fall down gracefully. You thought you could be full of emptiness. You wanted to unknow the known, and to know the unknown. You sought an intelligent, lucid ignorance. You wanted the reconciliation of the inner with the outer to be a comfortable, sane madness. You were trying to tread water, while still standing on the shore. You wanted to die in life, and to live in death. You wanted to attend your own absence. You wanted old answers, not new questions. You wanted nothingness to have context, but then it would be something, would it not? You wanted the spirit to contort into a recognizable form, but then it would not be spirit. You wanted separateness to be uncategorizeable. You wanted directions to the hidden treasure, but then it would not be hidden. You wanted only petty, swallowable, meaningless understandings, so you could continue in the world despite your inability to continue in it.

And a bird, with both feet held fast to a branch, flaps and flaps, curses and screams, and then forever assumes it can't fly.

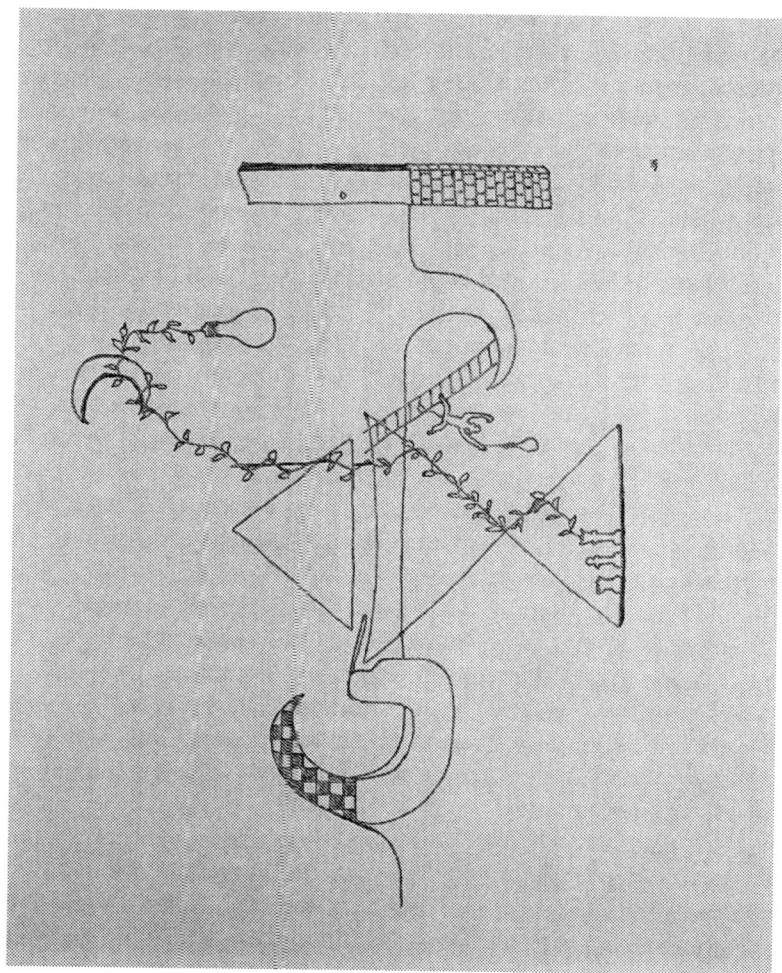

flying fish

You wanted to be shown a picture of it before attempting to construct the puzzle, but then it would not be much of a puzzle, would it? You wanted to have no interpretation, and you ended up having an interpretation of having no interpretation. You wanted to be without becoming, and to become without being. You desired only to do the doable, and only to know the knowable. You are afraid of not having what you do not have. You are afraid of having what you have. You are afraid to brood upon the mystery, to cast away the meaning. You have believed in your own untruths so thoroughly that to suddenly not believe in them would be tantamount to your own negation. That you dwell in the hypothetical, that you conjecture, ponder, and consider, does this not prove how little you actually know? Speculation is the physiognomy of ignorance. After all, would a being who 'knew', ever choose to surmise?

You dissipate into yourself, in whichever realm you falsify by accepting; in whichever realm you claim or dispute; in whichever realm you release or hold, hallow or despise. You dissipate alike within transience and eternity, hope and resignation. If you were outside of it you could destroy it, but you are irrevocably ensconced within it. You are it. Oh, you will never know, and you will never not-know. You live solicitously between the collapsed structures of two impossibilities. You will never know what you need know, and you will never unknow what you need unknow.

And yet, though you have swum blindly through the unknown depths like all the others, somehow, sometime, somewhere, suddenly something in you breaks through the surface, soaring into the immense, unliveable realms beyond all that is. In a breathless gulp of beingless rapture ...you finally have seen.

To gasp is to see.

Only the flying fish knows of the water.

destiny

Your first wish was so important and yet so fragile that it included the addendum that if you ever wished again, no matter how much or how hard, those wishes would never come true. And then you forgot your first wish, and its addendum. Therefore, though you now wish, and wish, and wish, and nothing ever happens, you never imagine that your wish has come true.

fate

A pole in search of a flag.
A 'what?' with no 'how?' to look for a 'why?'.
A blind man begging for sight in a lightless world.
A ringleader watching a circus.
A shadow chasing after a runner.
A feast waiting for hunger.
A bird flying after its wings.
If only we weren't what we aren't we could be what we are. But we are mere perspectives of ourselves; replicas of replicas. We walk in the shadow of what we are; we existed, but not really.

And yet it does not matter. For why should a flag, a magnificent flag- a glorious, anomalous, inexplicable flag- care if it was created, merely ...to make obvious the wind?

gnosis

What is it you seek anyway? To hold a truth within you? But perhaps the only truth is the uncomfortable emptiness which lies so irrefutably inside of you. And if poor you should choose to fill that honest vacancy, then your only truth will not be true, and, instead of being empty, you will be full of lies.

The understanding that you rest in is not yours; you do not know, you are known. A light is cast upon you and you claim to be not in darkness. But you are in darkness, the light has merely joined you there.

Every judgment you pass concretizes the false understanding you have of yourself, and binds you further into this tragic affair. You think to sever the mind, but with what? The knife would not fit the sheath, so you kept the sheath; you threw away the knife.

You want to lose what you have, you want to gain what you do not have. You imagine yourself as if trading what you have for what you want. But really you have nothing except want. And you are no match for the universe's skilled indifference. You try your best to haggle, but in the end you beg.

If you were a squirrel begging for stale peanuts in a city park, God would be a retired old curmudgeon with droopy jeans, who frequently smelled of whiskey, and was, on occasion, oblivious.

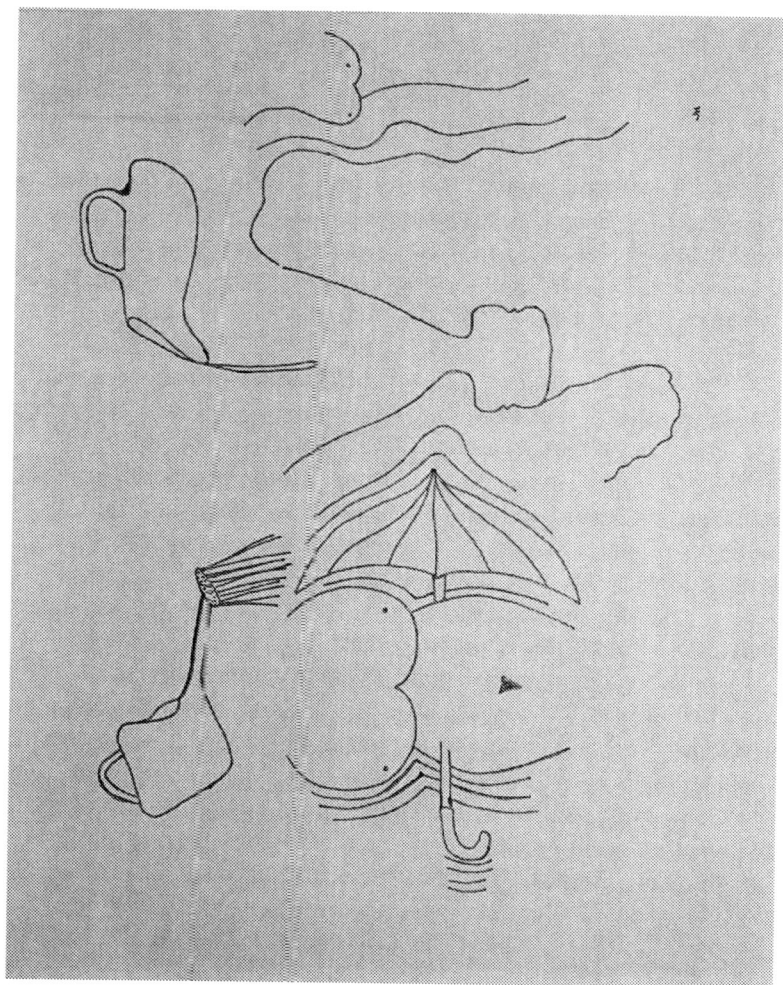

wisdom

You have sought for a person of knowledge your whole life, forsaking everything without exclusion: family, friends, health, and comfort. Your search has been exhaustive and all-consuming, but without fruition, until finally you learn the whereabouts of a true sage, and set off on your last, desperate journey.

Having extended yourself beyond your limit, you finally arrive at your destination, and with your weak heart throbbing, you enter the hidden hermitage.

Misery! There is no one to be found. You are distraught. And in the time it takes you to collapse under the stress of failure, another seeker, following the same arduous route as yourself, arrives to find you dying.

As he looks sorrowfully into your eyes you utter defeatedly "It doesn't make any sense."

Now, given all of this: given that this other person has also lost all that you have lost in the seeking, has also come the same distance and followed the same path as you, perhaps also knows only what you yourself know, and has also desired to find the same sage as you had sought, so as to right it all- does it matter that, as you resignedly exhale your final capitulative breath, you can hear the other person ecstatically declaring to you, "Master, I have found you, and your wisdom!"?

the tree

The Tree of the Knowledge of Good and Evil is the only tree which grows upside-down, with its roots in the air and its foliage buried in the ground. It is no wonder that its earth-bound, rotting fruit would be prohibited to tender, suckling, indigestive man.

To a blind person, suddenly seeing, even a pile of dog shit is a euphoric sight.

Indeed it was for mankind's sake that the forbidden fruit was forbidden; ignorance is our unchosen asceticism from the mind's insatiability. Knowledge would only lead to arrogance, and arrogance would lead to the most complete of solipsistic miseries. This is because 'understanding' is but a decadent downfall; by it we become gluttonous, insatiable beasts, machinating, and masticating, and turning salvation ...into sin; oh, how destructively we ingest, but do not digest, our course provender- our profane understanding. Thus it is perhaps essential to our beings that we do not know; because perhaps confusion is the hunger which keeps us from starving.

enlightenment

A man once awoke much more stupid and confused than when he had gone to bed. Unable now to reason correctly, he became anxious that this would be discovered and he would become a laughingstock, a village idiot. So he began studying texts, memorizing common phrases, and practicing confident eloquence.

Soon enough he was easily employing words and ideas his acquaintances used regularly. He remained bewildered for the rest of his life but continued on successfully with his previous existence. He died moronic and undiscovered. As did the rest of the world.

perspective

Beware of the smallest fragment of recognition, of conceptual acceptance. Hold that whatever allows you respite will conquer you forever. Chide the barren offering. Desecrate the soft ontologies. Disparage without postulation. Do not prop yourself up with myth or symbol.

Who can remember? Who can forget? Who can brave the loneliness of a mind divorced of all occurrence? Who can embrace what cannot be fathomed, by not fathoming? Not us, for we are the lame ones, sonorously bragging of our fancier and fancier crutches; pathetically we stagger, and then pride ourselves on what supports us. Set us upon our own two feet and we shall fall, and fall. Then let us fall. We must rely on nothing, expect nothing, and strive for nothing.

One must stand alone, stabilized by nothing the mind can adhere to, or one merely leans ...one does not stand.

One who is fed intravenously all his life has neither the ability to cook, nor to feed himself. Not even the ability to hunger.

One who seeks belonging in the world becomes a veterinarian. One who does not, becomes a dog.

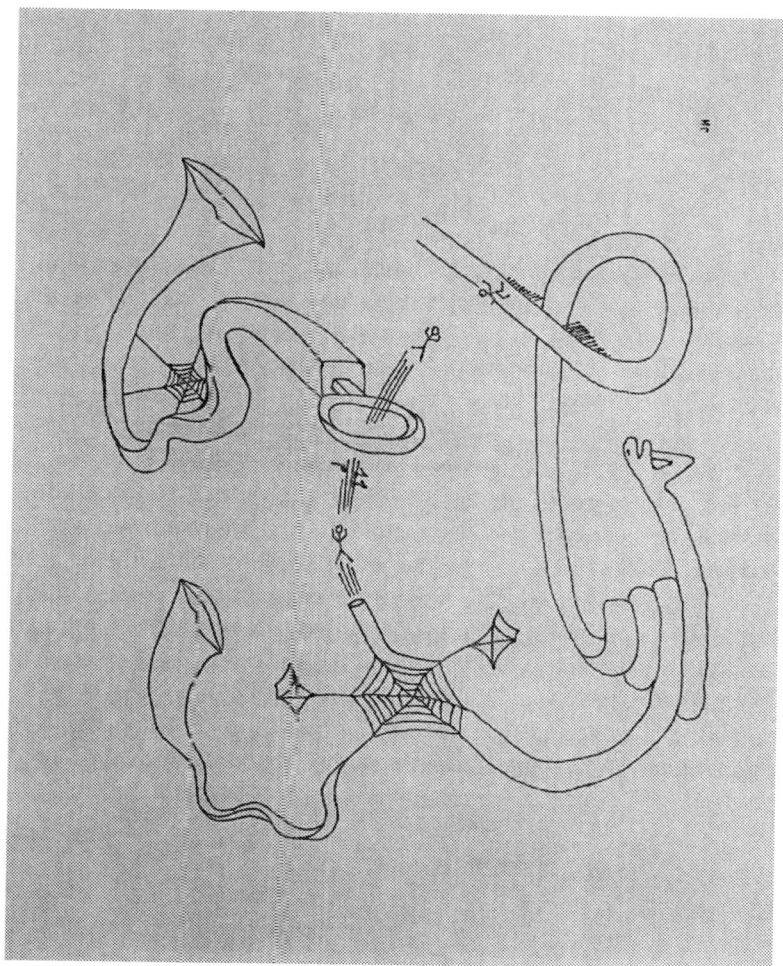

67

truth

Everyone is in a huge stadium, peering through binoculars which they have forgotten they are using, towards differing areas of the field. And since everyone sees different aspects of the singular show they all argue endlessly about what they see, and no one knows that everyone is right, and everyone is wrong.

Truth would not be irrelevant except that the truths one knows, because one knows them, are not as important as the truths one does not know, because one does not know them.

Know thyself? What more redoubtable impossibility could be set before mankind? What more humiliating project could one unwittingly undertake? It is as if the whole intention is to expose a person's inadequacy, for the best way to humble someone is to demand of them an impossibility; as if realization is but an amorous man, imagining away his own impotency, until stumbling, inadvertently, upon his wife's unmentioned dildo.

ignorance

You would not believe the truth even if you were told, so why should you be told? The movements of your being you will never understand. You writhe at the pinnacle of mankind's becoming. Your torment applauds the world for its complexity.

And you wonder why you dwell in the chaos and misery that you call ignorance. You dwell in it because it is there you have chosen to dwell; because in it you have not chosen to revel.

The wave does not require the shore.

You must accept that you are ignorant and that realization is still possible, or that you are ignorant and realization is impossible. Either way you must accept your ignorance. What is left, then, is only the necessity to accept that ignorance is possible.

The animal thirsts. The man drinks. The sage spits.

mind

The mind is a blind-man's cane, beaten ceaselessly upon the earth, until one imagines that they can see.

The mind is a grotesque feature; it reaches for what it cannot grasp, like a giraffe's neck, distended outrageously from seeking scant morsels ...just beyond.

The mind is not a weapon, but a shield. Though as such it does nothing to defend one from assault, but rather simply decorates a wall like a coat-of-arms hung desperately in plain sight; a dusty chunk of bric-a-brac, conspicuously placed to adorn the homes of living cowards who claim to be the progeny of dead heroes.

The mind is a falcon, but cannot be controlled by falconry. If this is attempted one realizes only too late that the call issued for its return is not that of a master, but a mole.

wonder

We venerate the way the blind man hears and the way the deaf man sees- because their senses become extraordinary through the compensation of a lacking. But we do not revere what the fool tells us of wisdom, nor what the idiot tells us of knowledge. No, we listen only to the seers- only to those whose vision is so clear that they have forgotten how hard it is to hear.

Isn't it possible that no truth explains the world as well as our honest questioning of it? When, etymologically, did awe-full become awful? And how much can we trust a culture that decides the astonishing ...horrid?

Is there not more wisdom in the helpless drool issuing from the silent, gaping mouths of wonderstruck fools, than in all the words, of all the wisemen, in all this wonder-parched world?

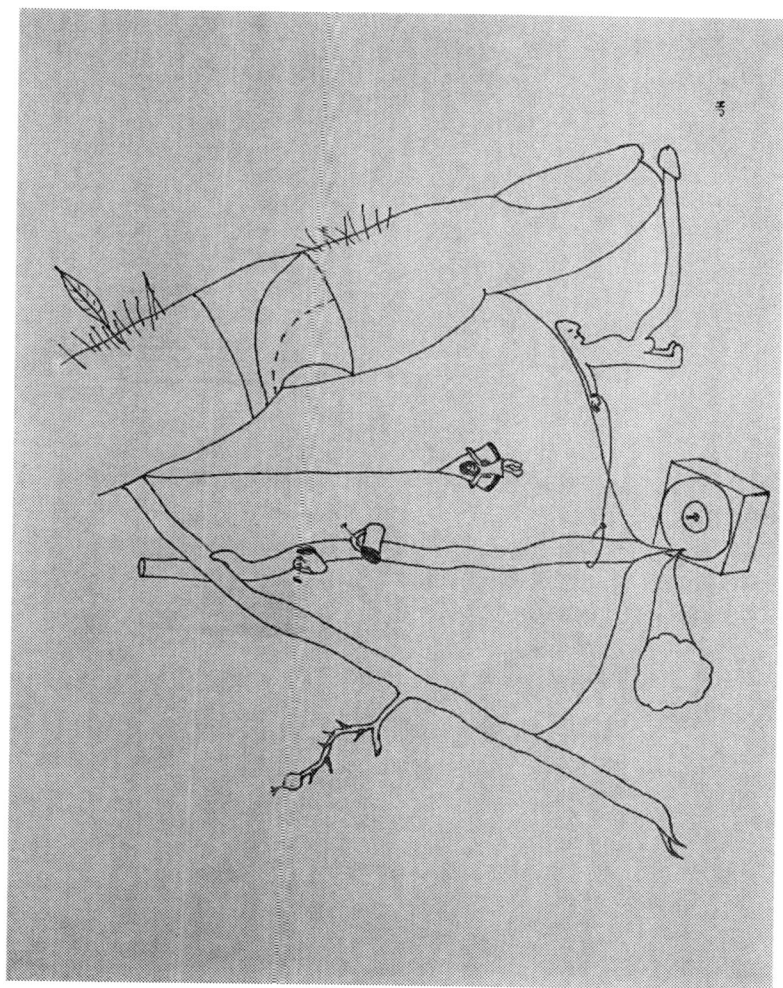

MUSE

the sermon

The preacher stands up, walks to the pulpit, looks softly into the congregation, rolls his eyes to the ceiling, gapes unabashedly into the distance, shrugs his shoulders, and overturns his palms, as if humbly saying "Who knows?". And the sermon is over.

The worm devoureth the core, and yet the seed flourisheth.

ecstasy

If you succeed in continuing, unobstructed, down those darkened, arduous corridors, which you have spent your whole life walking down in pursuit of light with which to light the dark corridors themselves, the same corridors which wither you to the bone, which dissolve all hope along the way, and from which you can never return- if those dark corridors lead you unexpectedly to an implausible precipice which you cannot go beyond but which provides an unimaginable, breathtaking view; if you struggle all that way- only one way out an infinite many- and you are left all alone- incorrigibly subdued by such an astounding, inconceivable, benediction- a lonely, foreign, spectacularness- never again to move from that spot, is it worth it?

The junky can, if nothing more, identify the substance to which he is welcomingly addicted. But the soul which rises and falls from an unknown cause; the soul which soars and crashes as if drugged by the hysteria of being; the soul which comes to love and cherish this ontological narcosis, what is it you would call its need? In which medium does it gleefully frolic, smashed about, caressed, and battered in the relentless, breaking waves?

Part IV: The Rubedo

"...I sighed because I didn't have to think anymore and felt my whole body sink into a blessedness surely to be believed, completely relaxed and at peace with all the ephemeral world of dream and dreamer and the dreaming itself."
Jack Kerouac

"...in the shaman's understanding...the dreamworld is the real world."
Robert Moss

"Those who lose the dreaming are lost."
Australian Aboriginal Saying

"You are your dream."
Eric Bennet (5 yrs. old)

*"Is **this** a dream?"*
John McLellan (3 yrs. old)

duality

The nature of the manifest is the same as that of thought, it is simply that one completely consumes the other. But which one?

The gross contains the subtle, the subtle contains the gross. Everything literal is also figurative, and everything figurative is also real.

Man exists neither in the world, nor in heaven. His shadow is merely cast in both directions, and he petulantly claims to be torn in two.

There is only subjectivity, thus there is only subject, thus there is no object, thus there is no subject.

An arrow, pointing towards another arrow pointing back at the first, points at itself without pointing at itself.

Just as a person whose hand is warm, feels tepid water as cold, and a person whose hand is cold, feels the same water as warm, so is duality the outcome of multiple perspectives of a singular event.

Just because something is not wrong, does not mean that it is right. That is where the dichotomy crumbles.

Perhaps it is the case that there are only two options: either 'a', or 'not a'. The question still remains- why 'a'?

There is no such thing as an egg, nor is there a chicken; if the antecedent requires a descendent in order to be, it exists not but in a cyclic phase. A skipping record never and always ends.

The beginning ends before the end begins? Everything is about everything else, in a tangled sort of way. There is no truth in limitlessness, there is only limitlessness. Nothing is specific. Nothing is differentness. No two perfect snowflakes are ever the same, and snow is always snow.

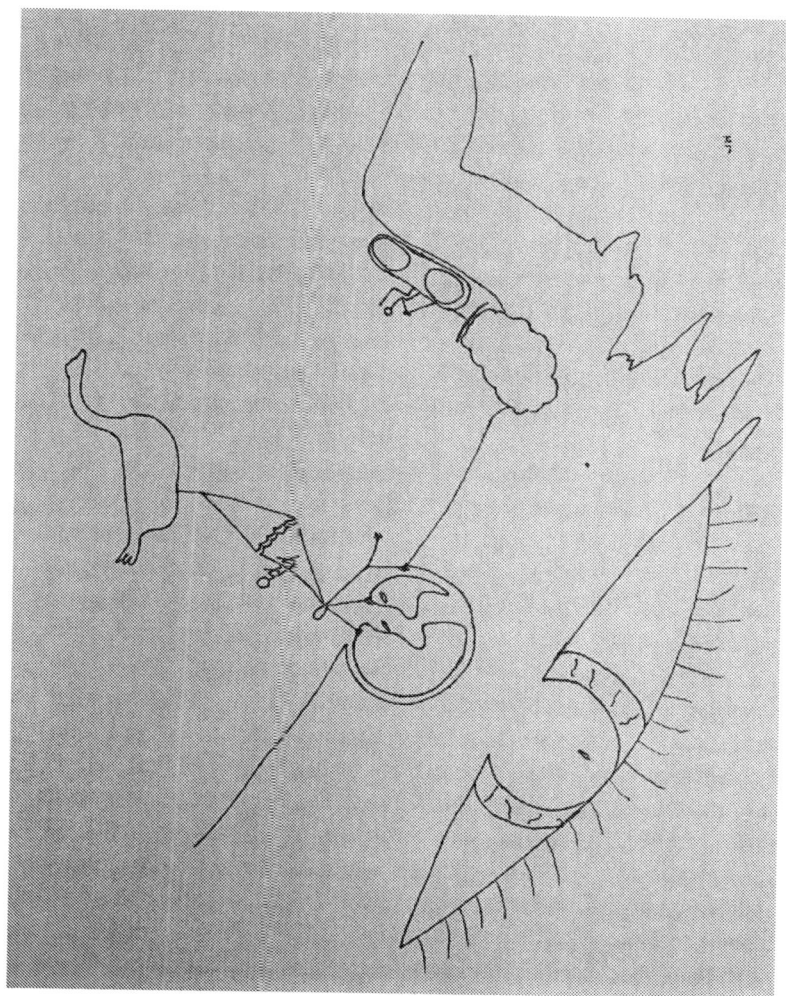

FEMALE

mirrors

There are naught but mirrors. And a mirror facing a mirror sees the nothing that everything is; sees itself not seeing itself. A reflection reflecting reflection; 'what isn't' facing 'what isn't'. Reflections are reflections.

Just as the individual is not divided, but is only a specific point of reflection to all else. A mirror mirrors that which it is not; it becomes by not being. In order to be it must not be. If it was something it would not be itself. If it was, it would not be.

Life is a stand-off between two men who have guns but no bullets, though neither knows of the other's true poverty. Bluff versus bluff is the battle. No one dies, and everyone's a killer.

A demon is the disbelief in itself; you need only accept that it 'is' ...and it ceases to be.

A dog unwittingly chases its tail. The tail, however, sees only a great, ferocious beast fanatically pursuing it. And even if the tail was informed of the continuum- that the beast is itself, confused- still it could not help but be terrified.

We need god because we do not need god. That is, because of our terror of the internal mystery, we authorize an enigmatic omnipotence to alleviate our own debilitating occurrence; god is the invention of our denials; we deny the incomprehensible within ourselves, forcing the mystery away, onto another, for 'to be', and to be a mystery to ourselves, that is too much for us; we transfer our unknowing, contriving an unknowable omniscience so as to conclude ourselves known; we invent a grandiose not-known to avoid the discomfort of our own ignorance; we point away from ourselves and comfortably gape, until mystery points back at us, and we realize that, all along, we have been captivated and looking at mirrors.

80

acceptance

The man who does not accept himself is a small man. Only acceptance is necessary to make him great. But there are actually no great men, there are only small men who have accepted such.

There is an inherent despondency which exists within an incident that cannot be confirmed as itself. That is: if an event is defined greater by what it will become than by what it is or what it has been, then man is not man.

The only spell cast upon one is that which convinces them that there is a spell cast upon them, when, actually, they are under no spell.

We are also our own hands, which sit quietly unattended, or respond without entreaty. No wonder we succeed at times- with such fanatics at our disposal.

It's like when you leave a baseball game in the 12th inning because you have become bored of it dragging on- you leave because of the same reason that you came- because of the baseball game.

To step away from being? Into the not-being that 'is'? But what of the not-being that is not? What of 'notness' and the ubiquity it implies? If being is the absence of nothingness, and nothingness is the absence of being, what then is the absence of absence?

The person who believes they are divine, is divine. The person who thinks they are not, is not.

The person who believes they are a child of god, is a child of god. The person who does not, is an orphan.

the kingdom

Not-being is born out of being. If you 'turn into' *IT*, you turn 'into' *IT*. What exists within a structure results from that structure. What exists outside a structure becomes itself a structure, and then results from itself. The Mother and Father are born out of the Child.

It is through the not-I that the little I, and the big I, are each other.

Thus the ante has gone up: one must be born twice again in this life; once again in body, once again in spirit. To be, *and* to witness being, this is the new requirement. To be the Dreamer *and* the Dreamed, which is to say, the Whole Dream. To be Whole.

To live in the paradigm, and live outside of it- in the known and the unknown; to be concurrently 'this', and 'not-this'; in *and* of, *and* not-of.

Everything is symbolic *and* real.

We belong both on earth and in heaven; hell is the distance between them.

Consubstantiation, however, is incorroborable, for who would say "I am the same as me."?

Indeed you have the fire in you, but that implies that you are the fire, and not as you just now suspected.

You need not seek the truth, you are the truth.

You need not pilgrimage through the forests, and deserts, and seas, tiring towards the kingdom; you are the kingdom, you need only now find the king.

oneness

Do not con-fuse yourself. You are infinite just as you are, without doing anything. There is only one event occurring; you are god's fantasy- that makes you god.

If you are not a separate being, why do you pretend to be separate? If you are a separate being, from what is it that you are separate?

What is related appears autonomous, and what is autonomous appears related; the related is autonomous, as in siblings not attached at the hip, the autonomous is related for the very same reason. Therefore what is related is autonomous and vice versa. Auto-nomy is merely self-naming amongst relationship. For what is autonomous must be related, or from what is it being autonomous?

If you would find yourself within the complexity, become the complexity, what then is there left to find?

God is the relationship of everything to everything else. Nothing exists alone- all is relationship. God is oneness composed of relation, from which the illusion of multiplicity emerges.

If you hold your finger twelve inches away from the front of your nose, and focus upon it, you see one finger. Then if you focus on the landscape behind it, you see two fingers. The two become one only when we look at the One. Oneness is merely a matter of recognizing its proximity prior to duality.

We are projections on the screen, projected by the projector which we are. We are created at every moment by the creator of every moment. Duality is the mind which sees the image as separate from the imager. Non-duality sees that they are One.

And yet, it is easier to clean a battleship with a toothbrush, than a toothbrush with a battleship.

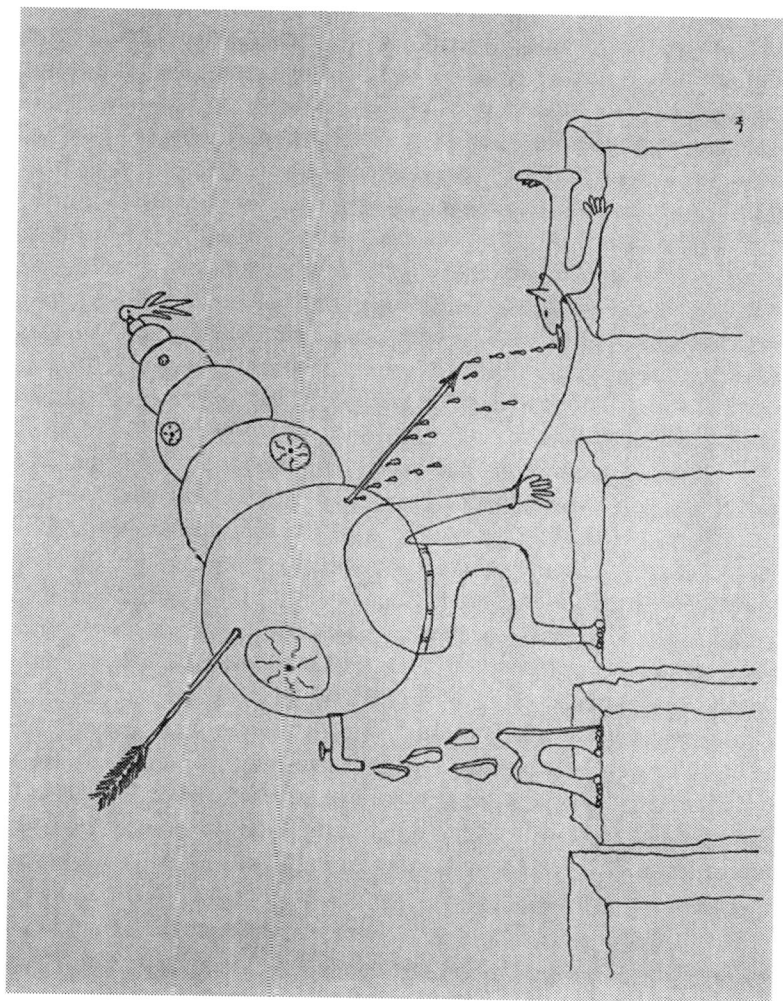

MALE

infinity

Does not existence, by its very implausibility, provide evidence for the assumption of infinite possibility? Isn't it logical that if infinite possibility did not exist- if there were limitations confining what could 'be'- then mankind would not, because of our implausible absurdity, exist? If there were, in fact, such parameters on existence- if what was possible also had to be probable- wouldn't more feasible phenomena occur before, perhaps instead of, the precarious ambiguity we call mankind?

After all, infinity does not embody everything, just a lot of things- an unthinkable number of things. And mankind occurs because of this default of immensity; because perhaps everything else more probable, or necessary, has already occurred, and yet there is still room; infinity allows superfluity; which is to say, certain things 'are' that need not 'be', and our 'being' is this gratuitous throng;

Occurrence does not conclude likelihood, after all. We fail to question what occurs, because it occurs. But why confine infinity to plausibility? Nothing is less plausible than what 'is'. In fact, to not occur- nothingness- seems far more plausible than what 'is'; in fact, what occurs does so, not despite but, because it is implausible; occurrence is implausibility. For if phenomena were commonplace they would not be, because only nothingness is commonplace; thus being occurs because it is less plausible than nothingness. And it is only because of this- because this life is but a singular occurrence within the infinity of possible worlds which may or may not be, that we can say that this life is 'right', for there is room for everything both possible and impossible within infinity; everything is therefore allowable, and at the same time nothing is necessary.

Therefore, because such a senseless, expendable periphery- man- occurs, this proves infinity possible; absurdity is the inductive measure. That is: infinity is not proven with a great many things, merely one; merely a possibility so improbable that, to accommodate it, limitlessness must necessarily occur, somewhere.

sameness

Though there is no argument which says of something that it should be what it isn't, an eternity of false knowings is contained in one instant of true ignorance. Awe is beyond time, though time is not beyond awe.

After all, from the paramount inexplicability of 'what is', we can deduce one of two possibilities: either we know that 'what is' is an absolute absurdity and hence know that it is implausible- such that its very outrageousness allows that anything is possible- or we do not know what this absurdity is and hence it could, beyond our wildest imaginings, be possibly anything. Thus, either anything is possible, or possibility is anything. Anything.

That is: the infinity of perspectives emanating from an improbable 'one actuality' are identifiable by their corresponding infinities of right and wrong, all of which, though relative, are absolutes; each reality is as true as true can be., and as false as false can be. Regardless, by the shear magnitude of these realities which are composed of partial perspectives creating time, man is trapped between what is relevant and what is irrelevant, not because they are different, but because they are the same.

qualitative mathematics

Infinity destroys all laws of mathematics, for at the point of endlessness, numbers are no longer quantitative but have instead become qualitative; infinity is a quality, not a quantity, for infinity plus one, or minus one, still equals infinity ($\infty+1=\infty$ and $\infty-1=\infty$). Hence infinity must be qualitative, for adding something adds nothing, and subtracting something takes nothing away. That is what is meant by limitlessness.

A dog, looking for the thrown snowball in the snow, hunts for the particular in the infinite, and finds nothing.

being dreamed

As if you had been having a lengthy, passionate, intense conversation on the phone with one of your closest friends, only to find out that you had been speaking to an answering machine all along, and the recording was somehow perfectly timed and in sync with the conversation you thought you were having; every sentence, every pause, every rejoinder and every nuance was responded to, supported, contradicted, ridiculed and all the rest, as if it were a true dialogue with a living, loving being on the other end.

How to explain this? What odd twist of fate, or what cold, omniscient deception has created and allowed this mystic madness to occur? And yet, what if every conversation you have ever had, whether live or on the telephone, was just as such? What if every acquaintance, friend, lover, sibling, or spouse, was simply a planned recording to make you believe you were not the only person alive?

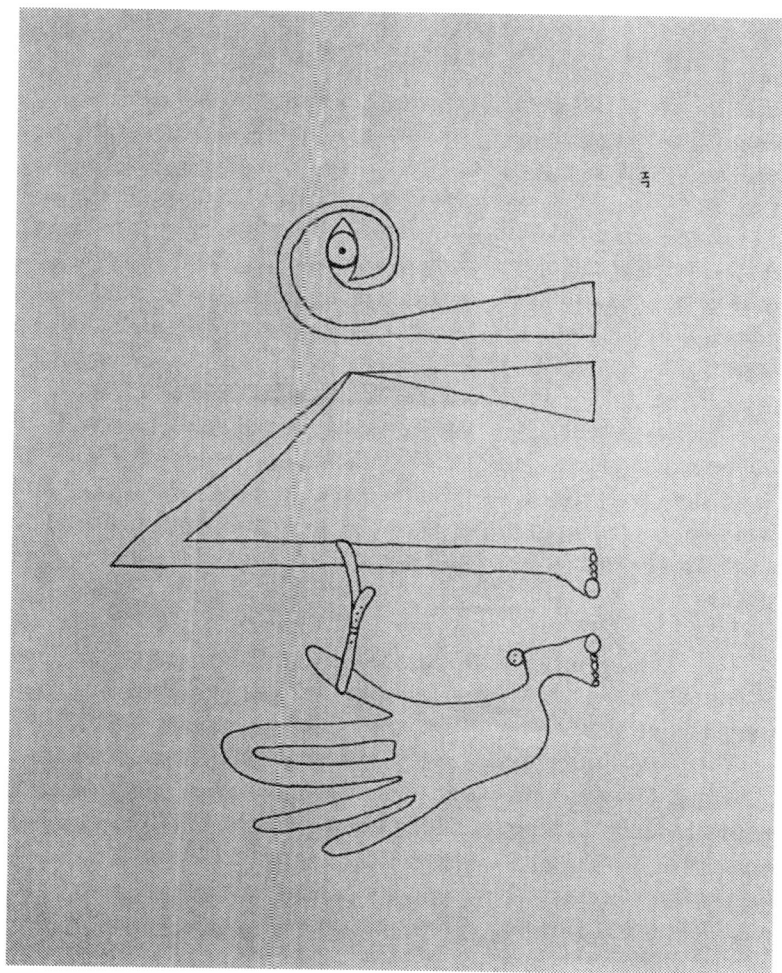

LOVE

the record

There is a tape-recording which never stops and so records everything that is always going on. And we can go back and listen to pieces already recorded, though while we are playing those pieces the original tape is still running. So the tape recording of us listening to the tape recording is also recorded. And then we can go back and listen to the tape recording of ourselves listening to the tape recording of ourselves. And so on. The whole problem lies in us becoming trapped in one of the layers of recording- who knows how far from the real movement.

Like endless levels of lesser rememberings, we may arrive at one plateau, still far from the source and the ending, and there decide to dwell, cyclically listening to ourselves listening to ourselves listening to ourselves, *ad infinitum*, and all the while somewhere else we're still actually living. Somewhere, but where?

Everything is Self, born out of, and overlapping Self, as if all of life is a divine, sublime palimpsest; we are God imprinted upon God imprinted upon God, and so on.

It is the multiple layers of reality, which emanate from the One, the singular event, which most confuses us, for each understanding, perspective, and vision must be placed within the context of the layer to which it applies, only then may it properly reflect the whole; to change layers, without altering one's vision, or one's understanding, is to become more lost in the new labyrinth which exists now only because one tried to improperly get out of the old one.

divinity

Perhaps neither subject nor object exists, but only the experience; 'experience' does not conclude an experiencer, nor an experienced event, it concludes only experience. Thus perhaps there are no 'things', only 'experience' which produces the experience of things. Nor is there presence, only the experience which produces the presence. One does not have 'experience', but in fact the other way around; the experience is independent of the subject, but not the subject the experience; experience produces the self, but not the self the experience. 'Experience' produces the experience of that which is 'experienced' and of the 'experiencer'. Though nothing but 'experience' 'is'. We try to invent an existence, an experiencer, out of experience, because we know that there 'is' something, but if that something is not-something, what is it?

We seek ourselves without, we seek ourselves within. And yet naught but a wily serpent could writhe upon this earth, and from that writhing . .move in a direction.

manifestation

What occurs, what manifests, first goes through consciousness before it occurs; 'what is' goes through us, before it becomes what 'is'; without us, this would not be. Time is consciousness forgetting that it has perceived occurrence already- before it occurred; occurrence is that which has been- it is the memory of what consciousness has forgotten. 'What is' is old by the time it becomes the newness called 'is'. Manifestation is consciousness requiring the reminder called occurrence in order to acknowledge what it already knows. If one perceives the manifest before it manifests, one need not perceive the manifest. From prescience to presence; life is an outcome- it comes out. 'What is' 'has been', though not in the form which it is. 'What is' is the last ditch effort of 'what need not have been'.

And yet, sound conceals the silence, but does not negate it. And where the parasite is found, there also the host will be.

incarnation

I

Like dysentery-causing amoebas, swallowed from the cold waters of a mountain stream, and then purged through the digestive system by heroic gulps of strong rum consumed by that wise, old, drunken mountain man, do we glide euphoric and high out of God's anus, with tales of our dark and mystic journey through the bowels of being, a sojourn which we again long to undertake, but there is no way back except to give ourselves again to the stream, and hope to one day again slake the thirst of our bitter host, home, and devourer.

II

We are eternally in God like a blindfolded man in a straight-jacket, who struggles and fights but cannot free himself. Yet he assumes there is other than darkness.

III

The wave is not independent of the water, though the water is independent of the wave.

The sun is more an oak than the acorn: independent of each other, the sun alone retains potential. The blinded acorn perishes.

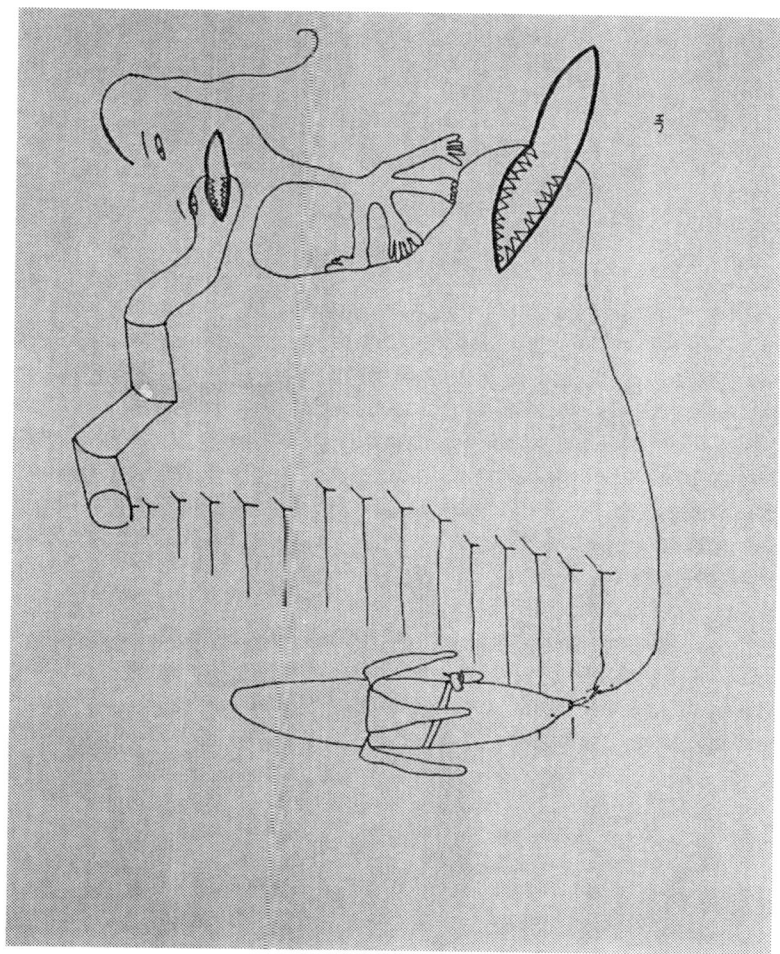

immanence

"Would the real god please stand up."
When this ultimatum is announced, man does indeed conspicuously stand up, but not until God first has stood; man hesitates nervously, and then, when God becomes obvious, man leaps up demanding that he instead is God. And so God returns to his seat, leaving man to stand alone in an empty auditorium with denial as his only witness. Then God sits again awkwardly inside a man, confused that perhaps all along he was not what he thought he was.

Angels know nothing of the angelic. The wizard cannot explain the wand. The child of God knows nothing of God, has never heard of God, says nothing of God, and can think of nothing that is not God.

logos

I

In the beginning was the word, the world, the semantic seminal semen, the unified verse, forming the university of the uni-verse, where there was no contra-diction, no scribbling scribes, no adversity from the adversary advertingly advertized. Only Lu-cipher de-ciphers Manu's manuscript of the Rama drama, by demon-strating stratification until we contend with the content which we formulate from the information of form; this was the vice of verse, or *vice versa*. For manifestation is the infestation of the festival of man; the reverberating verbiage of the illustrious illustrated illusions containing the sound bound wound. To compart-mentalize creates a cata-logos of logic, a cyclops called encyclopedia, a dementia of dimension, and a facetious facet, which desecrates the secret by ana-lysis of suppositorial suppositions in the diary of diarrhea; this is the sedition edition of the reason treason providing the Fall fallacy. Numbers numb the numinous. We do not liberate when we deliberate. Even awareness is a ware. We bathe in this bathos of mean meanings. The man-ager ages man. We regulate, speculate, and ululate. In interest we are interred in matter, in disinterest we are disinterred, since nothing matters. That is the oral moral of the mortal employment ploy. Remember the rage of courage.

logos

II

The earth is the hearth of the heart which hears with the ear without fear. Mater is matter, Pater is pattern. The parents are not apparent, nor trans-parent. The ghost is the host. Mater is the mate, the intimate maternal material, the *prima materia*, the primaddona, the matriarch matrix of the smothering mother, where every event is Eve tempting Madame Adam into the atom. Matter matters; the lapis lies in the lap- the rubedo's libido, flood of blood, is the menses consensus of the sacred red plant planet plan. The particle is the participant. The meat is where we meet. The spiral spirit is not the spiritual ritual, nor the gothic Golgotha; the *terra firma* terrifies the extra-terrestrial, begetting the hastening chastening. Heave ho to heavy heaven. The celestial celebrity suffers no dis-aster, for such is a master of another aster-oid. The tether is in the ether, the crucible in the crucifixion- an appointment with disappointing ointment. Hair is the air, feet are the street, eye is the sky. De-Sire is the Father of Fate, the Mother's other para-disiac aphro-disiac. Mammon is mamma the mammal, the beast from the east, the insidious inside of the animal animosity in the anima. Physis is the physician, the philosophia of Sophia. Here we are in Her, the omen of women. The flower flows, the rose arose. Ah, men! Amen.

logos

III

The sole son is of Sol. Hence solitude is solace amongst the sol-id, where there is a solution between Sol and Luna, despite desolation, and isolation, in the soliloquy of the solifidian soul. Ecstasy is not stasis. The incarnated are incarcerated, and the son is the song in pri-son. Hence the witch hunts in Salem, and Jeru-salem. Thus the coven of the covenant. Such was the naive nativity. Remember to reside in the residual. Perplexed in the plexus, you inhabit the habitual, the Empirical Empire, the carnivorous carnal carnival, described in the Manifesto of the Manifest, by which you avoid the void, and are a casual casualty of the causal; a hapless happy happening in which the tenant is an ant in the ill hill. The external is not eternal. It is this light which de-lights the knight in flight in the night. The Perpetrator perpetuates the accomplishing accomplice. For if God is good, and the devil is evil, and yet all is One, how can uni-one occur unless the con-fusion takes on the pro-fusion and brings about the fusion of op-posit-e posit-ions, I posit?

logos

IV

The 'I' is the 'Eye'. To sin is to be sin-gle, and not a part of the impartial, nor of the Imagination of the Imaginer, whose Image is the 'I' of the Mage. This is the severity of being several, the vision of the division of individuality's duality. The vice of service and advice. It is this density of destiny which produces identity. Thus sinful sincerity is the affectation of affection, which only polite politicians, vicarious vicars, gentile gentlemen, charitable charlatans, courteous courtesans, tormenting mentors, praiseless appraisers, adulterating adults, fiendish friends, and sophisticated sophists are arrogant enough to arrogate. The Id of the entity is the identity. Anger is danger; a Hellenic hell, and not the parade of paradise, which must be purged in purgatory under the influence of influenza. Injury is the jury where chronic chronos endures duration. Again is no gain. Tax is very taxing. The dollard loves the dolor of the dollar, for what is ex-pensive is not pensive. The miser is miserable; suffering the agony of no gonads, in the monetary monestary and the convenient convent. Tuition is the cost, intuition is the wealth.

logos

V

If we pursue purifying the purpose of our pernicious persons we allow the hallowed sacrament of excrement, thus sanitizing sanity. Increase the ease of the incredible edible. The supplicant is supple, and is supplied with supper. Succumb to succor and succeed. Amor is the amortal key to mortality. The fee is feeling. Faith is fate, destination is destiny, advent is the adventure. To be a-mazed, is to not be in the maze. To be a-mused is to have no muse. Do not ignore ignorance. Magnify the magnitude of magnificence. Now is wow. Applause for the implausible. The solute dis-solves in the Absolute absolution. To not attain, retain, maintain, detain, sustain, contain, abstain, or ascertain, is to have no taint. Always is all ways, whether it be with Allah, Kabbalah, Valhalla, or Shambhala. Allah-leuia. The parade of paradisiacal paradigms. You realize with real eyes, the now of knowing, and the heresy of here. Scared android turned sacred androgyne, orient yourself in the Orient, occur in the occult of the Occident. Grace is the race of humble humans. Attention attends, and has no tendencies. We forge on by forgetting. The way is not away, it is only a di-stance from the circum-stance of the circumference. Indeed, in deed. The center is where we enter when we concentrate on the motion of emotion, which is the dream stream, the momentous momentum of the moment of a good god go-ing.

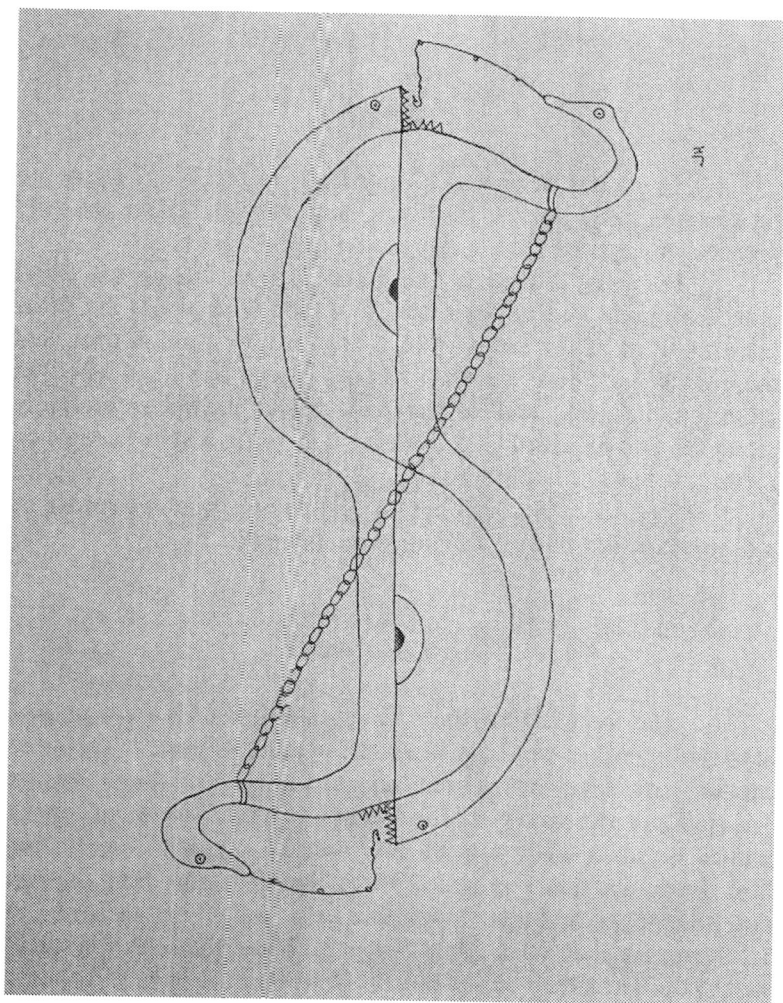

UNION

105

the whey

A barefoot man walks diffidently along the road of life looking for shoes, not life.

the way

There is a Way, but it only leads to the Way. There are no rewards, only delays; no oases, only mirage. There are only precarious stepping stones, there is no distant shore.

For what if God is like a person who lets an ant crawl onto their hand and up their arm, and then God places the other hand in front of the ant so that it crawls now up that arm, and then again back onto the first, as God places one hand after the other on the path, and so the poor insect meanders eternally along the two hands of God thinking it is going somewhere when actually it has not really moved.

Yea, there is a path but no destination; what we regard as a destination is simply ...fatigue along the path.

and the wei

The tools are all there. You can either lift them up and start swinging, or you can leave them there to rust. It seems to matter very little which you choose, when you have neither yourself nor the world to depend upon; when you have only a choice between what you are not, and what you will never be. But if you are going to swing them, by all means first sharpen and hone them, and then swing like hell. And if you are going to let them rust, then walk away, forget all about them, and let them rust. You can either be, or not be. And you are not, and totally accountable. Poor you. It isn't your choice, though it's you who has to choose.

106

the depths

Of course one retreats from the depths; one finds nothing there but depth. What did one expect? In the depths exists only undifferentiated, discomforting vastness ...depth. Everything certain is vague. One should keep to the shallows if 'finding' is what one is looking for.

It is a spot which does not sleep, does not want, and does not die. It is a spot hidden deep within oneself which one finally comes upon, is astonished, and then wishes never to leave. And so one never leaves. But if one could turn oneself inside-out, then that spot could roam, and one could go ...anywhere.

of spirit

At God's own speakeasy- which is a great tavern in the sky wherein every flavor of spirit which mankind has never heard of is served in the downy orify of amorous young wood nymphs, who are carried prone to your table on a carpet of fabulous humming birds- the Tree of Life supports the floating delirium, the tremendous delirium, the seat cushions are stuffed with the weightless feathers from the inner coat of resurrected phoenixes, a flying grand piano eternally improvises the music of the spheres, the Vestal Virgins perform a burlesque striptease on center stage, while saints drag mortal sinners up to the arena and flog them with jocular retribution, the Big Guy himself delivers the hookah to your table, sits down for a puff or two, blesses you and signs your limitless chit, the angels are bellboys, and Mary herself is our weeping concierge. Poor Mary, never stops that awful weeping. She always ruins everything. Makes it so uncomfortable. And yet, no matter. No one seems willing to leave. No place else to go. No chance. When you're called to the bar, you go to the bar, and you stay there. Despite the screaming sinners, the blinding lights, and that blessed old lady's chronic whimpering.

the garden

Unlike a living fence-pole- which sprouts new twigs every spring, and then is pruned back year after year by the Gardener whose intent is to keep the fence in good fettle, and to serve a greater purpose than letting a fence-pole become the tree it is trying to become and yet isn't, and also is, so that even that living fence-pole which is no tree is a tree groomed by the hand of the Gardener so as not to blossom and bear fruit, but only to prevent loss or theft of the succulent lambs within, waiting to be sacrificially slaughtered- unlike that fence pole you are the winter-bud born from withered roses, closed tightly in upon themselves. Your life is the sleep of flowers, not forgotten, in this cold, barren place, that to the Gardener, is still ...a garden.

the wilderness

If it was you who built this up, tear it down. If someone else built it, walk around it. If you cannot walk around it by all means go right on through, but take nothing from inside, smile occasionally, and remember to tell the children that it is sunny out today and they should forget their chores and be outside playing.

Truth lives out in the harsh, unfathomable, mindless wilds inside us all, and only hunger will lead us to the hunt, and to the game. And the game is a game, and play has no rules, and you are the wild horse who never was broken- who didn't need to be. You were corralled like all the frantic others, but you alone did not bolt, you alone did not buck. When the maddened rider first mounted, you moved not at all. And even as his crop beat relentlessly upon your flesh, you remained still, and then walked on your own way. You were not broken because there was nothing to break. No wonder they no longer confine you. No wonder you need not thrash to be free.

judgment

"Tell me of yourself", St. Peter inquired of the new arrival now standing before him at the Purly Gates.

And so the petitioner, anxious for entry into heaven, began an exhaustive explanation of the history of their life: of their likes and dislikes, their successes and losses, actions both good and bad, fears, transgressions and repentance, understandings and confusions.

When they were finally finished with this tiresome filibuster, St. Peter looked softly into their eyes and admonished: "You have informed me of everything that is not you, now tell me of yourself."

"But there is nothing left", answered the bewildered supplicant.

"Good", exclaimed Peter, "then you may go in."

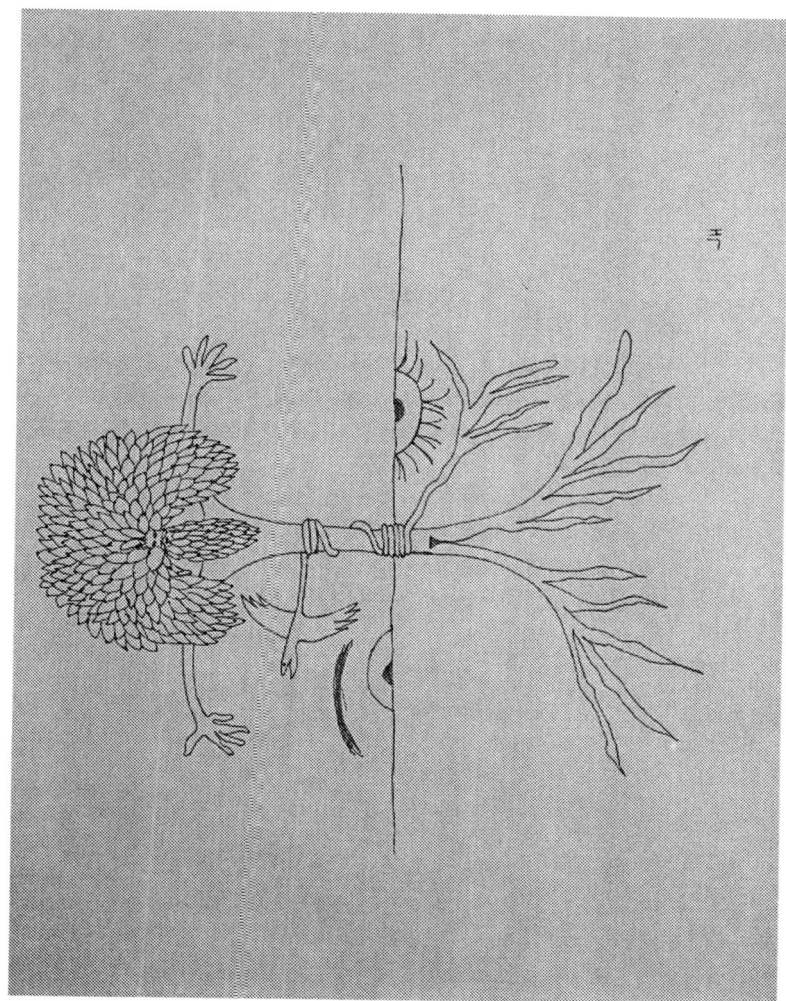

THE TREE OF LIFE

genesis

In the beginning was the Dream, and the Dream was God's dream, and the Dream was God, and the Dream descended into flesh, and the Dream was flesh, and the Dream dwelt among itself for eternity.

We meet in the silences, not in the song.

The flower does not seek the light, it is the light.

Time is the absence of God from your absent emptiness.

Life is a prayer, and you are *It* praying.

you

You are the dew, settling gently back upon that from which you were lifted. You do not deluge this earth like rain. You descend while we sleep, and rise before we wake. And whether you occur unnoticed or noticed, no one imagines that you eternally moisten ...what never dries.

eternity

Life is the flower and the bee; you are merely the pollen-sac, filled and emptied, emptied and filled; you are the unpleasant absence without which neither flower, nor fruit, nor bee, would be.

You are not the sun, nor the mist, nor the sight with which light is viewed; you are the rainbow, eternity's transience, born dimming miraculously away; here and not here, gone and not gone. You alone dissipate, while the sun, the mist, and the eyes remain.

Dreams end. What ends is a dream.

In, and Of : *memoirs of a mystic journey along Canada's wild west coast*

by Jack Haas

ISBN: 0-9731007-1-0

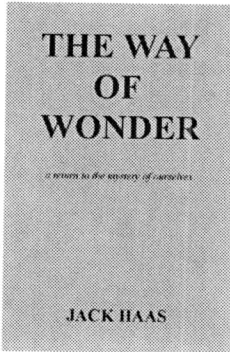

The Way of Wonder: *a return to the mystery of ourselves*

by Jack Haas

ISBN: 0-9731007-0-2

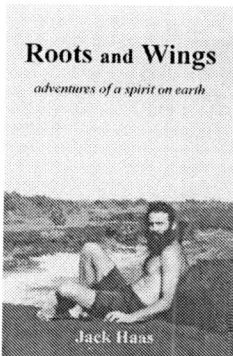

Roots and Wings: *adventures of a spirit on earth*

by Jack Haas

ISBN: 0-9731007-4-5

CPSIA information can be obtained at www.ICGtesting.com
Printed in the USA
LVOW101923291111

257010LV00001B/406/A